# Step-by-Step
# Papermaking

## David Watson

**Heinemann**
LIBRARY

**www.heinemann.co.uk**
Visit our website to find out more information about
Heinemann Library books

**To order:**

 Phone 44 (0) 1865 888066

 Send a fax to 44 (0) 1865 314091

 Visit the Heinemann Bookshop at www.heinemann.co.uk to
browse our catalogue and order online

Produced by Search Press Limited in Great Britain 2001.
First published by Heinemann Library, Halley Court, Jordan Hill, Oxford
OX2 8EJ, a division of Reed Educational and Professional Publishing Ltd.
Heinemann is a registered trademark of Reed Educational & Professional
Publishing Limited.

OXFORD   MELBOURNE   AUCKLAND   JOHANNESBURG   BLANTYRE
GABORONE   IBADAN   PORTSMOUTH NH (USA)   CHICAGO

Text copyright © David Watson 2001
Photographs by Search Press Studios
Photographs and design copyright © Search Press Limited 2001

The moral right of the proprietor has been asserted.

Originated by Graphics '91 Pte Ltd., Singapore
Printed in Italy by L.E.G.O.

ISBN 0 43111 170 7 (paperback)
05 04 03 02 01
10 9 8 7 6 5 4 3 2 1

ISBN 0 43111 160 X (hardback)
04 03 02 01 00
10 9 8 7 6 5 4 3 2 1

**British Library Cataloguing in Publication Data**

Watson, David
Papermaking. – (Step-by-Step)
1.Papermaking – Handbooks, manuals, etc. – Juvenile literature 2.Paper,
Handmade – Juvenile literature
I.Title
676.2'2

**Acknowledgements**
The Publishers would like to thank Alison Wright/Panos Pictures for
permission to reproduce the photograph on pages 4–5.

Every effort has been made to contact copyright holders of any material
reproduced in this book. Any omissions will be rectified in subsequent
printings if notice is given to the Publisher.

---

**This book is dedicated to my
daughter, Edie**

*My thanks go to the team at Search Press,
for their help and encouragement in the
making of this book – in particular,
Editorial Director Roz Dace, Editor John
Dalton, Designer Tamsin Hayes and
Photographer Lotti de la Bédoyère.*

• • • • • • • • • • • • • • • • • • • • • • • • • •

*The Publishers would like to say a huge
thank you to Rheanna Wood, Toby
Dowling, Lucia Brisefer, Victoria Bryant,
Jessika Kwan, Bradley James Murphy,
Luke Hunter, Abu Jahed, Liane Agnew and
Emily Malins.*

*Finally, a special thanks to Southborough
Primary School, Tunbridge Wells.*

When this sign is used in the
book, it means that adult
supervision is needed.

**REMEMBER!**
Ask an adult to help you
when you see this sign.

# Contents

# Introduction

Papermaking is one of the oldest crafts. It was accidentally discovered in China around 105 AD by Ts'ai Lun, an imperial court official. He noticed that some old rags that had been left out in the rain had been broken down by the continuous pounding of passers-by, and had eventually dried to a hard flat sheet in the sun. Old fishing nets, ropes and rags were later used to make paper. The photograph opposite shows a very basic form of papermaking in Nepal, which is similar to that used originally in China.

At first, paper was made for official documents and religious propaganda by the Chinese, Japanese and the nations of Islam. It eventually reached Europe around the twelfth century AD. The invention of the printing press in the early fifteenth century increased the demand for paper almost overnight. In Europe, the favoured material for papermaking was old rags that were bleached white. This tended to standardise the look of hand-made paper and make it appear rather bland. Some papermakers in places like Japan and Nepal continued to use a variety of plant fibres and as a result their hand-made paper looked much more beautiful.

When I was about ten years old I was given a sheet of European hand-made paper by my art teacher. It was yellowy white, quite stiff, with funny wavy edges that looked like somebody had tried to make it neatly but had not quite succeeded. The texture looked something similar to that of an old blanket and it had a funny smell. I really wanted to cut off those edges and make it look neat. I was told that it was very special and very

expensive. I felt so frightened of this piece of paper that I stuck it in a drawer, unable to use it for years and years. It is probably still there now.

Much later, somebody introduced me to a papermaker called Maureen Richardson and showed me some of her papers. 'That's not paper,' I said, 'it looks exciting, colourful and almost good enough to eat.' But it was paper. Maureen showed me how to make it

Alison Wright/Panos Pictures

*This Nepalese woman is using traditional methods to make Lokta paper from the bark of the Daphne or Lokta shrub. The bark is harvested, cooked, pulped and mixed with water. The mixture is poured into a wooden frame that floats on a pool of water. The frame is shaken gently to spread the pulp evenly, then dried in the sun.*

and I was hooked. I could not believe the difference between that and the old stuffy, smelly and frightening piece of hand-made paper I had seen when I was younger.

This book contains lots of exciting techniques and projects. The materials always come from recycled or reclaimed sources where possible, and most of the equipment can be found at home. This book is about breaking the rules and having fun, so let's get started!

# Materials

The best thing about papermaking is that you are recycling waste materials. Also, many of the things you need can be found in your own home.

Scrap paper can be used to make pulp. You can use coloured **pages from old telephone books** or pieces of **coloured cartridge paper**. For some projects you will need sheets of **tracing paper**.

A **mould** and **deckle** are items made specially for papermaking. The mould is a frame covered with a mesh screen, and the deckle is a simple frame, the same size as the mould. Both these things can be bought from craft shops.

You will need a jug for pouring water.

A **gravy baster** or an empty **squeezy bottle** are used when making multi-coloured paper.

**Old plastic cups** or **yoghurt pots** are ideal for storing small quantities of paper pulp.

The end of a **paintbrush** can be used to move coloured pulp around to create patterns or blend colours.

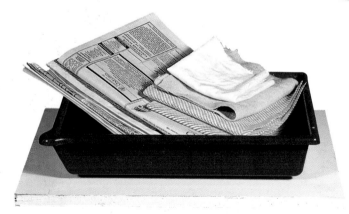

You will need a good supply of **newspapers**, a **shallow plastic tray**, some **kitchen cloths**, **old cotton sheeting**, an **old thick blanket** and **two wooden boards** to make sheets of paper.

Paper can be mixed in a **food blender** to make pulp. The pulp can then be poured into a **washing-up bowl**.

A **tea strainer** or a small fine sieve is useful for scooping up small quantities of paper fibres.

A **pencil** and **ruler** are handy for taking measurements.

A kitchen or bathroom **sponge** is used to wet the mesh screen on the mould.

**Plastic parcel tape** and strips of **foamboard** can be used to reduce the size of the mould.

Thin sheets of **acetate** can be used to make different shaped pieces of paper.

Use a **pizza cutter** to crease paper before folding it. You could also use the tip of a pair of round-ended scissors.

**String, cord, ribbon** and **copper wire** can be sandwiched between two layers of paper fibres. A small pair of **pointed pliers** will help you shape and cut copper wire.

**Acrylic matt varnish** can be used to make some papers look semi-transparent.

You can create beautiful paper if you add things to the pulp – **cut or torn pieces of paper, photocopies of photographs, leaves, petals** and **feathers** are all suitable.

# Techniques

The projects all follow the basic techniques shown here, with only slight variations. These techniques are based on traditional methods that are still used in hand-made paper mills today. Practise them until you are happy with your results, then you can start being really creative.

**Note** Exact paper quantities are not given. They will vary according to the type of paper that you are pulping. Generally, the more absorbent the paper is, the less you will need of it.

## Making pulp

Paper can be broken down into tiny fibres by blending it into a pulp with water. The paper fibres are joined together again to form new sheets during the papermaking process. The colour of the paper you use for pulp will determine the colour of the new sheets.

Prepare scrap paper for pulping by tearing it into 2.5cm (1in) squares.

Food blenders have very sharp blades. Always ask an adult to help you use one.

 Fill the food blender two-thirds full of water, then add a small handful of torn paper. Blend the mixture for approximately ten seconds.

**Note** Take care not to put too many pieces of paper in the food blender. You will know if you have because the sound will change if it is overloaded.

**3** Pour the blended pulp into a washing-up bowl half-full of clean water. Repeat these steps three more times.

# Making a couching mound

A couching mound is a base on which you make your paper. You can make a couching mound out of a pile of wet newspapers.

**1** Once you have prepared the pulp, you need to build up a couching mound. To do this, fold up five whole newspapers so that they are small enough to fit in a shallow plastic tray. Stack them in the tray, alternating the folds from one side of the pile to the other.

**2** Fill the tray with water so that the newspapers are completely covered. Leave them to soak until they are all thoroughly wet, then drain off the excess water.

**3** The couching mound should have a smooth surface that is slightly higher in the middle than at the edges. Press and rock the mesh screen on the mould across the top to make this shape.

**4** Place a clean kitchen cloth over the couching mound to cover it.

# From pulp to paper

This demonstration shows how to make one sheet of paper, but you can repeat the technique to make lots of sheets.

**1** Once you have prepared the pulp and the couching mound you are ready to make your paper. Begin by stirring the pulp mixture vigorously with your hands.

**2** Use a sponge to thoroughly wet the mesh screen on the mould. Then, hold the mould with the screen uppermost and place the deckle on top.

**3** Insert the deckle and mould into the pulp mixture, right at the back of the bowl. Take them down to the bottom, and level them out.

**Note** Steps 3 and 4 should be one steady, continuous movement.

**4** Pull the deckle and mould out of the mixture, making sure they stay level at all times.

 **5**

Carefully lift the deckle off the mould. Make sure that water does not drip on to the fibres, or your paper could be damaged.

 **6**

Turn the mould over then carefully position the front edge of the mould along the front edge of the couching mound.

**Note** Steps 7 and 8 should be one continuous movement.

 **7**

Roll the mould down on to the couching mound then press the far edge of it firmly into the mound.

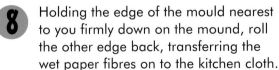 **8**

Holding the edge of the mould nearest to you firmly down on the mound, roll the other edge back, transferring the wet paper fibres on to the kitchen cloth.

 **9**

Place a clean kitchen cloth over the fibres, making sure that it is completely flat, with no creases. Your first sheet of paper is now complete. Place another kitchen cloth on top, ready to make the next sheet of paper (see step 4, page 9).

11

# Pressing and drying the paper

You may find it best to work outside when pressing paper. A lot of water will be squeezed out when you stand on the boards, and it can be quite messy!

 Place a wooden board on the floor and lay two whole dry newspapers on top. Carefully transfer your newly-formed sheet(s) of paper with kitchen cloths from the couching mound on to the dry newspapers.

Place more dry newspapers and another board on top, then carefully stand on the boards, increasing the pressure slowly. Add more weight by asking your friend or an adult to help!

 Remove the top board and the newspapers, then separate each set of two kitchen cloths, keeping a sheet of newly-formed paper in between. As this photograph shows, you do not have to worry about bending the sheets – by now the fibres will have joined together to form flexible sheets of paper.

Leave the sheets of paper to dry within the kitchen cloths on flat dry newspapers. Alternatively, you could hang them out to dry on a washing line.

**5** When your paper feels dry and rigid, carefully remove the top kitchen cloth – this should peel off quite easily. Insert your thumb under a corner of the sheet of paper and slide it along one edge to begin to remove it from the bottom kitchen cloth.

**6** Repeat step 5 on an adjacent edge. Hold the free corner of the paper in one hand and carefully peel the paper away from the kitchen cloth.

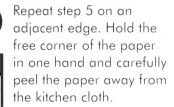

# Sparkly Birthday Card

Cards became popular during the Victorian period when the first festive Christmas cards were produced. You can now buy a card for almost any occasion. This birthday card is made using the techniques shown on pages 8–13, but small sparkly shapes and a person's age are added. The shapes bond together in the dried sheet and the image is fixed on to the paper as it is being made.

**YOU WILL NEED**

White paper • Food blender
Washing-up bowl • Plastic tray
Newspaper • Jug • Mould and deckle
Sponge • 2 wooden boards
2 kitchen cloths • Glitter confetti
Thin coloured paper
Tea strainer • Pizza cutter
Ruler

**1** Prepare some white paper pulp and a couching mound (see pages 8–9). Insert the deckle and mould into the pulp (see page 10), but rather than lifting them right out, bring them up level with the surface of the pulp and stop. Ask a friend to sprinkle glitter confetti over the deckle.

**2** Separate the pieces of confetti if necessary, then slowly lift the deckle and mould out of the pulp and allow the water to drain out.

**3** Carefully remove the deckle from the mould and turn the wet paper fibres out on to a couching mound. Tear some numbers out of thin coloured paper, then place them on one half of the wet paper fibres.

14

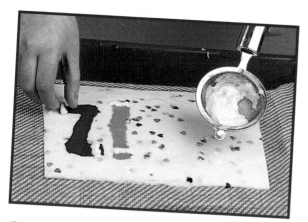

**4** Use a tea strainer to remove some paper fibres from the pulp in the bowl. While the fibres are still very wet, place a thin line of them across each end of the numbers.

**5** Cover with another kitchen cloth, then press and dry the paper (see pages 12–13). Use a ruler to mark the middle of the sheet then go over that line with a pizza cutter. Fold the paper in half to complete your card.

**FURTHER IDEAS**

Experiment with using seeds or leaves instead of glitter confetti – in fact, you can mix almost anything you like with the paper fibres.

# Fancy Folder

**Wonderful historical examples of patterned and textured paper can be seen in museums today. It is easy to recreate these effects using modern materials. Wire is used to make the design on this folder – it is bent into a design and placed under the wet paper fibres. Ribbons are placed between two layers of paper fibres. When the paper is dry, the wire is removed.**

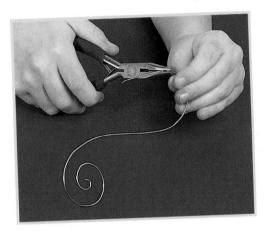

**1** Bend a length of copper wire into a shape of your choice using a pair of pliers. The wire shape needs to be small enough to fit on to half of your sheet of paper.

**2** Prepare some pulp made from cartridge paper, and a couching mound (see pages 8–9). Place a piece of old cotton sheeting on top of the mound.

**3** Place the wire carefully on to the sheeting so that the pattern will appear on one half of the paper.

**4** Take up a layer of paper fibres in the mould and deckle, then turn them out over the wire. Peel back the mould carefully (see pages 10–11).

Take up another layer of paper fibres then carefully turn them out on top of the first layer. Remove the mould, cover with another piece of sheeting, then press and dry the paper (see pages 12–13).

**5** Wet the ribbons then place them over the fibres, a little way in from the top and bottom edges of the paper.

**7** Remove the wire. Crease the middle of the sheet with a pizza cutter (see page 15) and fold it in half so that the raised pattern is on the front of the folder.

**FURTHER IDEAS**

Create your own patterns using different shapes — leaves, string or wire mesh. You can use anything that will make a mark.

# Personal Paper

Watermarked papers became popular in Europe during the fifteenth century. You can only see a watermark when the paper is held up to the light. The marks made were usually of animals and fruits or simple shapes like the 'C' shown here. Why not make personalised paper with your own initials?

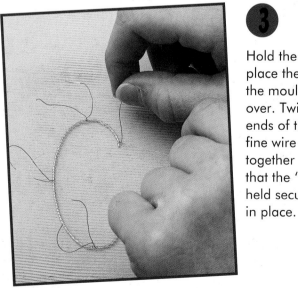

**1** Use pliers to bend a length of thick copper wire into a 'C' shape. Make sure it will lie flat on a level surface.

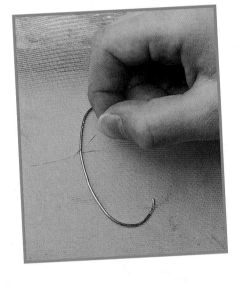

**2** Place the 'C' on the mould's mesh surface. Fold short lengths of thin copper wire in half then poke the ends down through the mesh, either side of the 'C'.

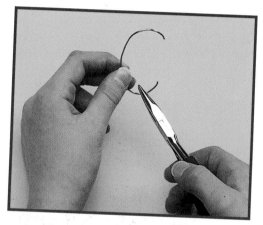

**3** Hold the 'C' in place then turn the mould over. Twist the ends of the fine wire together so that the 'C' is held securely in place.

**4** Make a very fine cartridge paper pulp by blending it slightly longer than usual (see page 8). ⚠

**5** Make a couching mound and cover it with a kitchen cloth. Take up a layer of paper fibres in the mould and deckle, keeping them very level as you remove them from the pulp (see page 10).

**Note** If you can still see the wire 'C', the pulp is probably too thin, so make the pulp slightly thicker and try again.

**6** Turn the paper fibres out on to the couching mound (see page 11). You should just be able to see the shape of the 'C' and there should be no bubbles or creases. Carefully cover the paper fibres with another kitchen cloth then press and dry the paper (see pages 12–13).

**7** Hold your paper up to the light to see the watermark.

**FURTHER IDEAS**
Bend the wire into different shaped letters (you could make your own name) or use it to create simple patterns.

# Feather Bookmarks

You can recycle all sorts of things and add them to the paper fibres – leaves, pieces of fabric, ribbons and more. Feathers are usually long and thin, so they make excellent bookmarks. This project allows you to make two bookmarks at once. You will need to prepare two bowls of pulp – one made from old printed paper and one from cartridge paper.

**1** Divide the deckle in half lengthways with a strip of foamboard.

 Prepare the two bowls of pulp and make a couching mound (see pages 8–9). Cover the mound with cotton sheeting. Dip the mould and deckle in the printed paper pulp, lift it out and let the excess water drain off.

**3** Remove the deckle then turn out the layer of wet paper fibres on to the cotton sheeting.

 Thoroughly soak the feathers in clean water, then place one on each half of the wet paper fibres.

20

Make another layer of pulp with the cartridge paper then turn the paper fibres out over the feathers. Cover this layer of fibres with cotton sheeting, then press and dry the paper (see pages 12–13).

**6** Apply a layer of varnish to the white side of the dry bookmarks, and watch the feathers magically appear.

### FURTHER IDEAS

Add other things to the paper fibres instead of feathers. Try using sequins, pressed dried flowers or sparkling metallic threads.

# Magic Picture Frame

Family photographs are often framed and displayed by proud relatives, or they are collected in treasured albums. If you have a favourite photograph you can show it off in this vibrant frame. Get an adult to help you colour-photocopy the photograph before you begin, making sure it is slightly smaller than the mesh on the mould. Two colours are used for this frame, and it combines magically with the photograph without you having to use any glue.

## YOU WILL NEED

Coloured paper
Food blender • Washing-up bowl
Plastic tray • Newspaper
Cotton sheeting • Jug
Mould and deckle • Sponge
Plastic parcel tape • Coloured acetate
Photocopy of a photograph
2 wooden boards

**1** Prepare one colour of pulp and a couching mound (see pages 8–9), then place a piece of cotton sheeting over the mound. Scoop up a layer of paper fibres and turn it out on to the cotton sheeting (see pages 10–11).

**2** Place the photocopy of your photograph on top of the wet paper fibres.

**3** Thoroughly dry the mesh screen on the mould, then stick strips of plastic parcel tape round the edge.

Cut a piece of acetate slightly smaller than the photocopied photograph, then place it on top of the mesh and hold it there with your thumbs. Prepare a second colour of pulp then dip the mould (without the deckle) into the pulp. Level it out under the surface, then carefully lift it out. The pulp will settle around the edges of the acetate.

**5**

Carefully peel the acetate away from the paper fibres to leave a border.

**6** Turn the border out over the picture. Cover with another piece of cotton sheeting then press and dry the paper in the usual way (see pages 12–13).

**FURTHER IDEAS**

Choose different colours for your border, and add glitter confetti or pressed dried flowers to the paper fibres.

# String-Along Book

You can recycle old paper to make this beautiful book, which can have as many pages as you like. The paper has a great texture and is perfect for chalk or pastel drawings, or you can simply write on it with a pen. You can make front and back covers for the book using thicker paper if you wish.

**YOU WILL NEED**
Coloured paper
Food blender • Washing-up bowl
Plastic tray • Newspaper • Jug
6m (20ft) of strong, thin, textured string
Mould and deckle
Old thick blanket
2 wooden boards
Sponge

Prepare some pulp and a couching mound (see pages 8–9), then place a piece of old thick blanket on top of the mound. Turn out a layer of paper fibres on top (see pages 10–11). Thoroughly wet the string then cut it in half. Arrange one end of each length of string on the paper fibres as shown.

 Turn out a second layer of paper fibres over the string to complete the first page of the book, then place two pieces of blanket on top.

Make the first layer of paper fibres for the second page of the book. Take the string across the couching mound, leaving short loops on one side. Make the second layer of paper fibres then turn this out over the string.

**Note** This stage can be a bit tricky, so do not hurry it.

**4** Continue making more pages, moving the string from one side to the other, until you have made about ten pages. Lift the wet paper fibres and blanket layers on to a wooden board. Put another board on top and press out all the water (see page 12).

**5** Place the pressed pile at one end of your work surface. Ask a friend to hold the bottom page down, then carefully open out the linked pages. Put dry newspapers below and on top of each page to soak up the moisture. Remove the pieces of blanket when all the pages are dry.

**FURTHER IDEAS**
Make the book into a large wall hanging by linking more sheets at the top and bottom as well as at the sides.

# Funny Face Lampshade

This project shows you how easy it is to make your own lampshade. The pulp you will use is made from tracing paper. This has very short fibres, and all kinds of strange things happen as they dry. In fact, it is just about impossible to keep them flat!

Electricity and water can be very dangerous together. Ask an adult to disconnect the table lamp from the electricity supply before you start this project.

### YOU WILL NEED

Low-energy light bulb, maximum 15 watt
Table lamp base • Tracing paper
1m (3½ft) of stiff copper wire
Pliers • Sticky tape • Food blender
Washing-up bowl • Plastic tray
Newspaper • Jug • Mould and deckle
Sponge • Old thick blanket
2 wooden boards

 Take the copper wire and place the centre of it against the lamp fitting. Carefully wrap it once around the base of the fitting.

 Loosen the wire carefully from around the base of the lamp fitting and remove it, taking care not to alter the shape. Use the pliers to bend the rest of the wire into an interesting face shape. Make sure the neck is at least 7.5cm (3in) long.

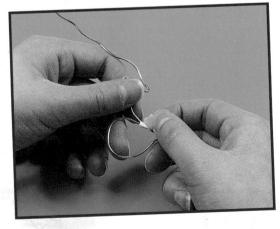

 Join the two ends together with sticky tape.

Place the wire shape over the first layer of paper fibres, leaving the neck end free.

Prepare some tracing paper pulp and a couching mound (see pages 8–9), then place a piece of old thick blanket on top of the mound. Turn out a layer of paper fibres on to the blanket (see pages 10–11).

**Note** The tracing paper pulp should be finely blended for this project.

Turn out another layer of paper fibres over the wire shape. Carefully place a second piece of blanket on top, then press and dry thoroughly (see pages 12–13). Ease the wire back over the lamp fitting then bend the paper up in front of the light bulb.

### FURTHER IDEAS

Try making different wire shapes such as stars and moons, and add glitter to the paper fibres so that the lamp shade sparkles in the light.

# Pulp Painting

You can create amazing paintings using pulp made from recycled coloured paper – swirls and circles of bright colour can be combined or blended to make abstract or realistic designs. The colours will lighten when they dry, so use really brightly coloured paper to make your pulp. In this project, the pulp is not diluted in a washing-up bowl. Instead, it is poured straight into the mould and deckle which sits in a shallow tray of water.

**YOU WILL NEED**
Coloured paper
Food blender • 3 plastic cups
2 plastic trays • Newspaper
Jug • Mould and deckle
2 kitchen cloths • Sponge
2 wooden boards
Paintbrush

Prepare three different colours of pulp (see page 8) then pour each colour into a cup. Make a couching mound (see page 9).

**2** Place the mould and deckle into a shallow tray. Fill the tray with water until it is almost level with the top of the deckle.

**3** Hold the deckle down to stop it floating off the mould, then pour one colour of pulp into the deckle, starting at one edge.

**4** Add another colour of pulp, leaving a space between the two colours. Add the third colour in the same way.

**5** Use the end of a paintbrush to blend the colours together so that there are no gaps or holes. Add more pulp if necessary.

**6** When you are happy with your picture, carefully lift the mould and deckle out of the water. Allow the excess water to drain away, then continue making the paper as shown on page 11. Press and dry the paper (see pages 12–13).

**FURTHER IDEAS**
Make more colours of pulp and use them to paint a simple landscape.

# Patterned Paper

In this project you can recycle your paper to create vibrantly coloured patterns. A gravy baster or an empty squeezy bottle can be filled with coloured pulp and used to squirt out designs and shapes. The pulp has to be blended finely so it does not clog up the nozzle of the gravy baster. It will be just right when it looks and feels like soft ice-cream.

**YOU WILL NEED**

Coloured paper
Food blender
Plastic tray • 4 plastic cups
Gravy baster
Mould and deckle
Kitchen cloth

**1** Make up four colours of pulp (see page 8) then pour each colour into a cup.

**2** Place the mould in the tray and thoroughly wet the mesh with a kitchen cloth. Position the deckle on top of the mould.

**3** Squeeze the end of the gravy baster then dip the nozzle into one of the colours of pulp. Gently release your hold to draw up the pulp.

**4** Move the gravy baster over the mesh then gently squeeze the end so that the paper fibres flow from the nozzle on to the mesh. Continue until you have covered it completely.

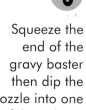

**5** Clean the gravy baster with water. Change to a second colour of pulp and start painting your pattern.

**6** Continue adding the colours until you are happy with your pattern.

**FURTHER IDEAS**
Make a simple picture using this technique – try a boat on a stormy sea, a dinosaur or a fantasy landscape.

**7** Leave the paper to dry naturally on the mould, then carefully peel it away from the mesh.

# Index